"The table of contents for *This poem
kills fascists* reads like a long poem, in
which the reader might fill in the
blanks. Of course it is not. TRT is
known for his short, pithy, poems,
and in this collection they are darts
to the heart of their target."

-Donna Hilbert, author of
Enormous Blue Umbrella

"There are so many reasons to admire Thomas R. Thomas. He is a man of caring and quiet morality. He is a person of understated grace who does not care for the spotlight. He is a man who helps his family and his neighbor, and his neighbor might be anyone who is alive and sharing this world with him. Beyond all else he is a man of principle. Along with all of that, he is a fine and talented poet whose work I read over and over. With the tyrant at our door, Thomas has turned his considerable talents to speaking the truths that need to be spoken about those who desire fascism to become the norm. This collection shines light on the evil that has always been present in the United States of America and has begun to accelerate. I'd follow Thomas with his moral center anywhere. This collection is brilliant. As Thomas writes in this book, "let the poets ring the bell of truth." He has done so."

-John Brantingham, author of
Gone Back to Wild.

"Like driving a classic sports car on the open road, shift, speed and freedom are embodied in these political poems by Thomas R. Thomas. "Breaking News" display road signs that distract us with roadside attractions and "alternative" routes, or they point us forward relentlessly without a rest stop in sight. (People of color know this all too well, freedom of the open road was a promise unkept.) On the analog radio of real life, we are "clap-trap blasted… by sheep bleating nonsense words without meaning." Thomas demonstrates the mental effort to make sense of the road we are on as political forces wreck familiar streets or obstruct the flow of the American culture of destination, setting up roadblocks on the Constitutional freeway approaching Democracy."

-Mary Torregrossa, author of
My Zócalo Heart

Also by Thomas R. Thomas:

Star Chasing,
Five Lines,
Missing Shaun,
The Art of Invisibility,
In Which the World is Turned
Upside Down,
If Wishes Had Wings and
Other Stories,
Schrodinger's Cat

This Poem Kills Fascists

Thomas R. Thomas

Luchador Press

Big Tuna, Texas

First Edition: 1 3 5 7 9 10 8 6 4 2
ISBN: 979-8-89975-047-2
LCCN: 2026940035

Cover image: Thomas R. Thomas
Author photo: Thomas R. Thomas

Table of Contents

Forward

This Poem Kills Fascists is Thomas R. Thomas' reaction to the tragic first year of Trump's (and his handler's) second, and far worst take-over. Liberty stands weeping; Justice ignores the heavy thumb; pigs fight for position feeding at the public trough. That is the Kleptocracy that is today. Brownshirt Proud Boys, Oath Keepers and Boogaloo henchmen mask as immigration enforcement, opposing voices are silenced, shadowy forces pull the strings of congress—this is only the first year of occupation. Next years mantra: "Damn the consequences, full steam ahead."

While most others in the arts run for cover, try to hold onto their fellowships and grants, hide behind a camouflage of distraction and indifference, and add to the spectacle, Thomas R. Thomas is different. He pulls no punches, doesn't sugarcoat reality with allusions to a great by and by justice. *This Poem Kills Fascists* voices expresses the horror that is each morning's headlines. He joins resistance voices from the past who stood up to fascism: Paul Éluard, Nelly Sachs, and Pablo Neruda.

On my first birthday my father was absent, crossing the Remagen Bridge with the 1st Army, and then going on to assist liberating Nazi labor and concentration camps. I grew up in the shadow of his stories, spoken and unspoken. I think of past lives shattered and lost in defense against fascism, present lives displaced as political theater, only to find the movement again alive and well. The poems in *This Poem Kills Fascists* are raw, unvarnished songs against the clear and present evil before us.

—Kendall Johnson
December 12, 2025,
Author of *Fireflies For These New Dark Ages*

This Poem Kills Fascists

the silenced are bleeding

we now envy

our loved ones who have

passed from this life

hope
is missing—where
has she gone

she is now purged

from the tomes of love

her future is erased

evil resides within
the hearts of the few
captivating the fools

today we dwell
within despair
then we fight

why is the sun
still shining when
my heart is black

tainted soil
spoiled by the
touch of greed

the desolation of

the land is now

upon us

shame revisits
us we cannot escape
the stain of

our past when
there is no admission
of our guilt

the blood of the
innocent cries out
as their bodies

sway in the
breeze below
the black sky

the erased
believes
she is

equal
to
he

the privileged
are now enabled
by his twisted

lust for power
free now to torture
children they

imagine are
less than human
with threats

hiding behind
a wall of vapid
anonymity

the fascist turns
on his right stands
the billionaire

on the left
his book of lies
he smiles

accuse the
innocent despise them
for their name

obscure the
truth so your black
heart is hidden

purge the voters
but be sure to
remove

them if their name
is Latin or Arab and
no concern

if they are
a citizen
or born here

or contribute
to society
or are kind

74 million
they know he's
a liar—a cheat

don't believe
the lies he tells
are complicit

in his crimes
will one day say
I didn't know

he told us he
was our salvation
the blood is

on all
of their
hands

sheep bleat nonsense
words without meaning
claptrap blasted

across the airwaves
determined to abuse
the fools ears

. . .

draconian deportation
rooted in fearhate of the other
ignoring the damage

damage to the innocent
victims of your vitriolic hate
damage to yourself

damage to those who
believe you understand
care and love them

when you are
incapable of any
care

the world is fragile
the world is burning
war in Ukraine

war in Middle East
and he will now throw
gas on the world

the divider in chief
the purveyor of hate
imagines he will

unite the country
by removing everyone
with a dark face

everyone who disagrees
with his plan of evil gain
all who truly love

the innocent, the meek
the merciful, the ones who
act like Jesus

who the evil one hates
then those who bow to him
will be one with him

Steven Miller hopes
he can carry out his life
long goal to rid

this country of all those
he deems inferior to him
and his kind

his kind which is
a black hearted non-soul
this Heinrich Himmler

exudes hate
loathes love
lives death

the first thing the
exnew president will do
when he becomes

the exnew president
will be to pardon the
the gentleman

Whitey Bulger, who'll
be so proud he will certainly
be crying from his grave

Breaking News:

It is now revealed that the planets, sun, moon, and stars really do revolve around the flat Earth, in a circular motion. This will be proven to be true once the exnew president will be sworn into office (finally), the public education system will be abolished, and the new non-science will be established and taught in all of the private Christian schools (now funded by the US government).

This has been brought to you
by the newly formed non fourth
estate now trustworthy only news
service Truth Social News.

it's exciting to learn
that the recent election
was prophesied

in the Bible, look it up
Proverbs 26:11
you'll find it enlightening

this sick exnew president
picks his sickophants who think
they run the country

yet are too afraid to
act on their own, so they are
puppets on the strings

he pulls so he can dismantle
the country he loves to hate so
he can rule them all

the bobbing heads
not those who are in his pocket
the mainsteam media

as they listen to all of
his sickophants who blather
evil nonsense

yet
act as if the evil is
valid

not speaking against
all the crimes they breath
have abandoned

the fourth estate
live for entertainment
so it is time to

let the poets ring the bell of
    truth

tRump appointees
so incompetent it proves
his unfitness

proves his intention
to crumble the country
at the foundation

you can see the
strings that run directly
to our enemies

under the spell of the
misogynist megalomaniac
voters believe ignorant

promises will enrich
yet will in truth impoverish
and still will point

at those who desire
honestly to provide for them

tRump has a plan
for tanking the economy
evict illegal aliens

but only those
with dark skin and
legal aliens and

any legal citizen
that became naturalized
or was born here

if they have dark skin
then place tariffs on goods
from Mexico and Canada

then blame the high
prices on Biden and Newsom
while he eats

cheeseburgers made by
minimum wage… oh wait he
evicted the cheap labor

poverty rather
than pay a living wage
spend billions

to steal from
medicare, social security
medicaid

and laugh at us
as they stuff their pockets
with the money

we
create for
them

this, a simple test
does the so called christian
love Christ

to the evangelical
who worships at the feet
of the billionaire

You cannot serve God and wealth

those who will rule
this land who love riches
and power, hate

mercy and charity
you knew this when you
supported them

so you hate Jesus
if you have read your bible
you are guilty too

swimming in hypocrisy
Mitch McConnell opposes
banning polio vaccines

too bad he also
received the vaccine
for sympathy

if only he would get
the vaccine for greed
or have a soul

77,303,573
can't be wrong
if you lie

to the world
uncountable times
if you try

to overthrow
the government
you wouldn't

do it again
just because you
are a rapist

a thief and
a known conman
a failure

77,303,573
can't be wrong
right?

*"The disaster
'could have been'
caused by DEI."*
—PResident Donald ꟻRump

blame DEI
transparent
racist trope

citing no
evidence
spreading

his
usual
hate

we now have a
criminal president
who ran to avoid

prison, always
arguing like all
criminals

that he is
fully innocent
of truth

now is the time
for predators and abusers
to be praised and loved

a president who has
no respect for women
raping women

a famous writer
who steals words from
the mouth of women

in league with our
president by raping women
denying truth

now is the time

for predators and abusers

to be praised and loved

tear down these walls
dismantle the structure
pile drive the foundation

we destroyed the essence
of the institution of
our government

we mourn
its passing
on this day

we imagine
resident Rump
to be the

Sauron in
our real fantasy
yet this

wicked little
so called man
is truly

the mouth of
Sauron—the insipid
Stephen Miller

there's a cruelty
in special knowledge
the pride of

knowing a tiny thing
that only the important
people own

then puffing up
their chest and calling
the ignorant stupid

immigrant Elon
is bribing federal employees
buying their jobs

crippling the
federal government
then filling

their jobs with
tRumpy sickophants
blind drones

taking down the
federal government
so he can fill

the void
with his evil
plans

immigrant Elon
is spying on our
personal files

invading
our privacy
so tRump

can cancel
our Social Security
Medicare

attack us
if we challenge
his evil

Resident Rump
has handed the keys
to the kingdom

to acting
treasury secretary
immigrant Elon

who has now
robbed the vault
all the money

in the US
as we admire this
Trojan horse

for those who think
Resident Rump can be
managed, will have a

safe presidency
you need to remember
that the last 4 years

his festering boil
of hate—his sense of
justice that he

the god of the universe
has been grievously wronged
and must be avenged

he considers his election
a mandate from his very own
Mount Olympus

this deranged creature
will rain terror on all of his
puny enemies

he does not care that the
world will suffer from his rage
we will all suffer

Resident Rump is bent
to purge the FBI of agents
he deems disloyal

remove talented agents
who sit on the frontline
protecting us from evil

especially the evil
from within our borders
like Resident Rump

This poem kills fascists

the fools on the hill
are turning a blind eye
as the Resident in the.
White House dismantles
the government—steals
our personal information
fires all competent
government agents all
workers who are not
loyal to the Resident
replacing them will
his loyal sickophants
who

are as incompetent as
the Resident and will
by their failures let
the wolves into the fold
we are in full danger mode
the war has begun today

this poem is not over...

imagine when
Resident Rump
talks—whenever

he opens his mouth
all of the reporters in his
presence interrupt

"I need to tell you
'sir' you are an idiot
we can't do that"

Medicare and
Social Security
are paid by

me and my
employer for me
not by taxes

the federal
government are
stewards

of my money
terribly poor
stewards

they have stolen
it through the years
and will never

pay it back
if they deny my
rights to claim

my payments
and coverage
then they

Resident Rump
senators congress
Elon Musk

are criminals
and should be
convicted

attention whore

Resident Rump's sole purpose
to be resident is to get revenge
on his perceived enemies, also
because he is a rabid attention
whore. His other evil schemes
are the agendas of the rats that
run his cabinets. Of course,
we all knew what his evil plans
were. His voters knew, but
hated the Democrats, loved
his evil plans, or thought they
were voting for Donald Duck.

Dachau
is in the news
and it's no surprise

to those who know history
but to those who don't
you need to know

history repeats
itself when we look
away and let the evil grow

DOGE

Department of Government
        Excising
eliminating all government so
only Resident Rump

is the government
destroying all opposition
then only the autocrat is left—yet

the autocrat that is left in power
will not be the fool on the hill
Resident Rump

the gauge whether
a company or person
is afraid or in league with

Resident Rump the terrorizer
is that they will follow
his evil or stupid

vindictive edicts
where Google Maps
calls it Gulf of America

or Amazon cancels DEI
We are now 1933
Germany

cancel DEI
now protections
for women

gays anyone
white supremacists
hate

are gone
rape and murder
are protected

again

the fascist in chief
Resident Rump
banned

an AP
reporter
from the Oval Room

because the AP called the
Gulf of Mexico by
its true name

now the
Fourth Estate is
gagging itself in fear

stand up—speak out for

the true and fearless

free press

ifwhen
Resident Rump
takes away our Medicare

our Social Security which
belongs to us
then

my wife
will die I will not
know when my next meal

mortgage gas electric breath
will come my will
to live…

Resident Rump
is now denying the
people who arrived on

this land before all of us
the right to be
citizens

next
deport them back
to all the reservations

which is impossible since
how do you deport
them if

they are
part European
(no other people count)

and if they own land—that's
OK since that is part
of the plan

also this
white supremacist
wants to purge the land

Karoline Leavitt
the other mouth of Sauron
only spouts the lies of Resident
    Rump

the current lie is against federal
    judges
doing their constitutional
job of challenging

the illegal actions
that Resident Rump is signing
that are robbing people of their
    rights

we have the right to challenge
        every
action by the Resident he
is not king

For Sale:

Free reign as acting president,
and unlimited access to take
down the government.

$277 million

Free access for ICE to raid
churches, synagogues, homes,
and use of NYPD.

drop charges for all crimes

Need insane diseased conspiracy
nut to take away all health care
rights from all Americans.

    must be billionaire. will
    bleed future funds.

Alternate Universe

I finally realized that I am in an
alternate universe where good
is evil and evil is good. Now
I understand why so many
people believe that Resident
Rump is the messiah, and that
his racist and nihilistic views are
wonderful. Now where is the
door to the beautiful universe?

there is a coup
right now fomenting
this moment in the office

of the president—beware
Resident Rump and
his clown car

of co-conspirators
are violently attacking
the structure of the government

dismantling all protections
of the people who
depend upon

the form of the
constitution to live
we are dying and we have let

the devil
in the
door

universal healthcare isn't
more expensive
it's cheaper

all your money
goes to healthcare
and cuts out the high profit

it eliminates the billionaire
and passive investor
we all benefit

now is the time for hate
a perverted form of christianity
where

everyone
feels free to judge everyone they
think is less than them

celebrating murder and
starving the poor—love the rich
loving

money
turning backwards all the teaching
of Jesus Christ

it's 1933
Germany again
but will we learn

this time from
history or
will

we fall
to the spell
of an evil fascist

every rich man
sweats the sweat of
one man

the greater
his billions the more
sweat and blood

is paid by the
humble the rich despise
the lower

the person
in the world's estimation
the greater the

humble

to those who say
I voted for Trump three times
now DOGE took my job

they say now I hate
Trump and everything that he
stands for

goodness
and love, grace and mercy when
your heart is not broken

is true righteousness
give mercy and grace to a stranger
freely

we are now
in the era of the dismantling
of the United States

it was a good
experiment even with all of
its flaws

it is sad
to live in the time of its demise
we mourn its passing

the ultra wealthy
can have their overabundance
they seem to

need this
feeling of power over little people
humility is not theirs

for myself I am
happy to have the elusive riches of
enough

yet
if they persist in stealing our enough
beware

the assault on the
federal employees slashing their
livelihood

will not save
money but will create such havoc
the world will be crippled

the economy will shatter
the only ones to benefit will be
the rich

yet
they forget that the foundation
of their wealth is

those who they hurt and
as the world crumbles under them
their wealth

evaporates
they will be crushed under the feet
of those they despise

hate is rampant
now immigrants are denied
    admission
on the pretense of imagined

infectious disease without
any test except of where they are
    from
rooted in

racist hate
we are now following the blueprint
the xenophobic model

laid out 100 years ago
we have had good relations with
    our
neighbors

sharing
labor, trade, and peace, to our benefit
why cut our throat with hate?

today is the day
mark the now on all
of your calendars

Donald Trump
will never be satisfied
he will declare

himself to be
the royal president
for life

and it's true
those who raise the
flag the highest

who imagine
themselves to be the
most American

will fight the hardest
for the most un-American thing
King Trump

indiscriminate pilfering
of federal employee's jobs
=
mass chaos

tRump
in Putin's pocket
fighting to own Ukraine

to own their mineral rights
is too stupid to know
this will ignite

a world war
his wealth will
evaporate and he will meet

the fate of Hitler, Mussolini
all evil men who lust
for corrupt fame

guns

the Republicans have said all along
no restriction on gun ownership
now want to take guns from the
mentally ill. They will then define
mentally ill as so called sexually
deviant (LGBTQ+), antifa, liberal,
progressive. Also against any
foreigner, or anyone who says
anything against tRump.

For Sale: America

for a mere 5 million dollars
(none of those
lousy Euros €, Pounds £, or
   Yen ¥)

we want anyone with the money
especially
those with a criminal past

we don't want anyone
who is poor
and can actually work at a job

for this you can be a Gold Card
citizen
and a one day president

I am in mourning
my nation has been murdered
I have torn my clothes

cast ashes on my head
I can only mourn for the morning
I must get up

clean myself
the murderer must be exposed
stripped naked and shamed

then astounded confused
with articulate and organized words
truth will burn

his unholy skin
he will for uncounted
    generations be
a curse we will avoid forever

tRumpian

English is now the official
language of the USA. This is
done to ignore and isolate non
English speakers, and it is rooted
in racism. Which variation of
English is official? Should we only
allow the way we spoke it in the
18th century? Which one of the
30 major dialects should we speak?
Should we force the people who
speak Gullah English to speak
"proper" English? Should we
forbid the Amish and Mennonite
people to speak German?
Shouldn't we call this national
language American, or maybe
tRumpian?

don't imagine
Trump is not working for Putin
since he has severed

all ties with our allies
and lined up his agenda with Russia
this is not

so difficult
the Republicans are not any longer
Red, White, and Blue

but now they are the
Russian White, Blue, and Red
this subtle

shift is not

so difficult to imagine—their fake

Christianity is rotten

now is the time
for the new Enron to shine
fraud

crime
are now applauded since
a crime lord now

runs the country
we are now in a golden age
of evil

for some
when the wash of wealth
    drowns them
it clears their soul

of empathy, replaces
sympathy with the black tar of
    hostility
all who

they think
are beneath the crush of their feet
deserve no mercy

this is as if they
are immune to the crushing arm of
justice

the key
to Donald Trump—if he speaks
he's lying

if he accuses
someone of a sin then that is his
crime

if he
is trying to run the country like
a business he

will make the
country like all of his businesses
a failure

then

blame the failure on anyone else

but him

we live
on three legs
solid stable secure

remove one leg and
we topple to the
ground

remove
two legs and we
cannot stand alone

the destruction our
union is sure
on one

the sign of civilization
is not because one man has great
wealth

power
over many lesser people is a sign
of evil and greed

there are no lesser
people unless that person devalues
life

Trump
and all his cronies
drunk with imagined power

think they will now begin
their thousand year
reign

yet
justice reigns
as it always does in the end

and will turn to be a thousand
day reign at the
end

we live
on three legs
solid stable secure

remove one leg and
we topple to the
ground

remove
two legs and we
cannot stand alone

the destruction of our
union is sure
on one

imagine
the college rapist who gets
away with his

crimes because
Daddy doesn't want to ruin his
future

and now
he has always gotten away with
his crimes so

now he is the
president, thinks he is invulnerable
who now is

ruined?

so

if we all now buy American
first, does

that mean
we can buy from all of America
no

It just means
we buy from things made only
in the

US
we can't buy cars, electronics
for some no

electricity
now the candle business will
boom

we will
all be walking everywhere
reading books

and praising the
president for all the winning, yet
no jobs

how soon will
the new Hitler create
martial law

Trump manipulates
the market so he can profit—fully
aware

he is
destroying the economy, and we
lose everything

there'ssss a

ssssnake in the henhousssse

(it'ssss Trump)

Trump buys
the Supreme Court (tell me I'm
    wrong)
then

bans
all law firms that oppose him from
    all
federal courts

give me your weak
ass argument that he is not
    crippling the
court

he's
making his move to be the
   supreme
dictator

all nine justices
ordered Trump to return the
    innocent man
to the US

of course
he defied their orders in his
    arrogance
a declaration of

a dictator who
has proven he will never give up
    the power
he craves

it's a crime
one hundred sixty five years ago
we

died
over a hateful evil ideology
don't pretend

it was for the
sovereign rights of the states
to

be
free if the oppression of the
federal government

now the ideology
of the administration of Trump
is

no

more than an evil power grab
from the most vile

people on earth
who have no love for anyone
and

my
family is now divided over hate
just like before

Trump is
threatening and will deport US
attorneys who

defend immigrants
send them to El Salvador prisons
this is

the start
of the evil administration's turn
to become the

despotic ruler
and the end of the US
    democracy

now

we

will be next because we oppose

this evil

the Trump tariffs
put most US businesses out of
business

they can't
run their company in the US
without major cost

the only ones who
will survive are the super rich
who

will
be glad to swallow their small
competition

anyone
who comes to the US is in
danger of arrest

for no reason
everyone needs to keep
away

we
are now the most dangerous
country

Stay Away!
US citizens are now in extreme
danger

Resident Rump
barely lives in the White House
rarely

works
no, never has worked in his life
shadow villains

rule the country
leading the president on puppet
strings

why would I
want to protect the immigrant
gay

bi
trans person when I am not one
myself

because
being pro DEI means I am
    following
the

bible
that you only read when it
    validates
your beliefs

this is what
the parable of the good Samaritan
means

the free press
is strangled, on the verge of death
they

need
to now be on the attack for the
    truth
or be complicit

with the enemy
who are running this country
to

the
ground

denying the
lower courts the right to rule on
birthright

citizenship
prevents them from ruling on any
constitutional

right, this
gives Resident Rump dictatorial
power

Thomas R. Thomas publishes the small press Arroyo Seco Press. Publications include *Carnival, Chiron Review,* and *Silver Birch Press.* His books include the art of invisibility, *Star Chasing, three on a wire, Missing Shaun,* and *If Wishes Had Wings and other stories.* His website is thomasrthomas.org.

This project was made possible, in part, by generous support from the Osage Arts Community.

Osage Arts Community provides temporary time, space and support for the creation of new artistic works in a retreat format, serving creative people of all kinds — visual artists, composers, poets, fiction and nonfiction writers. Located on a 152-acre farm in an isolated rural mountainside setting in Central Missouri and bordered by ¾ of a mile of the Gasconade River, OAC provides residencies to those working alone, as well as welcoming collaborative teams, offering living space and workspace in a country environment to emerging and mid-career artists. For more information, visit us at www.osageac.org

Osage Arts Community